When Flowers Bloom

By Liz Fiedler

Illustrated by Dan Mondloch

ISBN: 9780578908625

Written by: Liz Fiedler
Illustrated by: Dan Mondloch
Book Design by: Colleen McLaren

Josh

Your legacy will live on forever.

Vidalia

This story demonstrates so many of the things your father was determined to teach you — hard work, patience, and the importance of helping those you care about.

Baby

You were loved and wanted more than words can say by both of your parents. This story is a testament that God gets to choose the timing of things. The day after the funeral, I found out you were joining Vidalia and me on this journey. We can't wait to meet you.

For every thing there is a season.

We can try to understand,
 but only God knows the reason.

We can try to plan.

We can try to prepare.

But God decides Who, What, When, and Where.

Someday we will know why.

Vidalia and Daddy helped Mommy put some seeds
in the ground.

First you dig a hole, and then top it with a mound.

Some flowers need more time, so we start them
in a pot.

When spring is here, we move them to their
permanent spot.

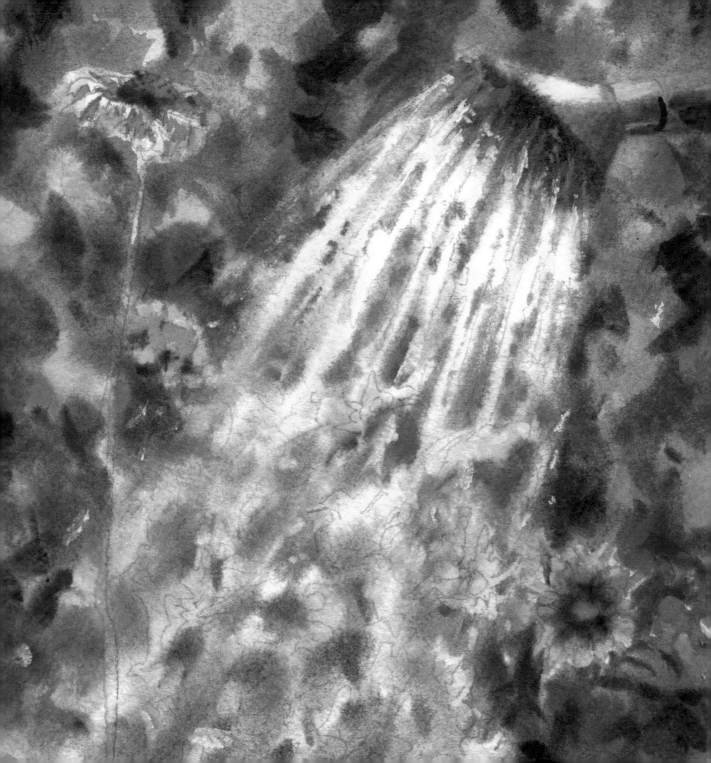

Flowers need water, like all living things;
from people to dogs to birds with wings.

Vidalia started to spray the leaves on top,
when suddenly Mommy told her to stop.

To grow best, we need to water the root.

Make sure you aim the hose by your foot.

We pick the flowers and put them in a vase.

Sometimes, we even tie on a ribbon with lace.

Knowing when each flower is ready to pick
is sometimes quite the trick.

Put your money in the slot
Don't have correct change?
Just give what you've got.
Settle up the next time you stop.

Weeds are a problem that start out small,
but we shouldn't delay or ignore.

If we let them get too big, removing them is
much more of a chore.

The problem with weeds is they block flowers
from the sun.

Flowers without blooms are just no fun.

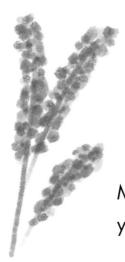

Mommy told her helpers that some flowers
you pick when the stem doesn't wiggle,

And trying each one made Vidalia
and Daddy giggle.

Other flowers you pick when they start
to bloom.

If you're lucky, you can have a vase full
in every room.

16

If you pick one flower too soon,
or another too late,

you won't see them at their best
and you might have to wait.

God gets to decide the timing,
and when flowers look their best.

When they finished, they decided
to take a rest.

At the end of the summer, Mommy told Vidalia that the best flowers need to be left to grow.

We can't pick them yet, or next year we won't have any seeds left to sow.

We let them bloom and dry, and save the seeds,

but just the flowers, not the weeds.

23

It started to get colder, and the leaves began
to fall.

Vidalia got worried, and said, "We have to
save them all!"

Mommy told her it would be alright,
and even more fell through the windy night.

The tree just continued to let the leaves go,

and soon it started to snow.

27

April showers bring May flowers, it is true.

Waiting all winter to plant the garden is
not easy to do.

If we want to have beautiful flowers
in every room,

we have to be patient and know
God picks when they bloom.

About the Author

Liz Fiedler is a part-time Nurse Practitioner, part-time Flower Farmer, and full-time Mom. After the unexpected loss of her husband late in 2020 due to a heart attack, this story came to life. Liz found the timing of the garden comforting, and it inspired her to write this book. Liz lives on her late husband's family farm in Central MN, and her daughter Vidalia is the sixth generation to live there. Their second child is due August 2021. The Flower Farm is named Sunny Mary Meadow, after Josh's mother, Mary, and her sunny personality. It thrives in honor of Josh. For more information about her Flower Farm and other inquiries, visit www.sunnymarymeadow.com

About the Illustrator

Dan Mondloch is a Father, gardener, and landscape painter living in Central Minnesota. For more information about the artist, visit www.danmondloch.com